This book
belongs to

...........................................................................

# THE SUPERNATURAL

Written by
**Jon Day**

Edited by
**Fiona Mitchell**

zigzag

The author, Jon Day, is a world class professional magician and has written a wide variety of books for children. He is a member of London's Inner Magic Circle and has appeared on television.

ZIGZAG PUBLISHING

Published by Zigzag Publishing,
a division of Quadrillion Publishing Ltd.,
Godalming Business Centre, Woolsack Way,
Godalming, Surrey  GU7 1XW, England.

Series concept: Tony Potter
Managing Editor: Nicola Wright
Senior Editor: Helen Burnford
Senior Designer: Nicky Chapman
Production: Zoë Fawcett & Simon Eaton
Designed by: Ross Thomson
Illustrated by: Hemesh Alles (Maggie Mundy Agency),
Peter Bull, Peter Dennis (Linda Rogers Associates),
Miranda Gray (Maggie Mundy Agency), Justine Peek
(Kathy Jakeman Illustration), Roger Stewart.
Cover Design: Debbie Chadwick
Cover illustration: Simon Dewey

Color separations: Sussex Repro, Brighton, England
Printed in Singapore

Distributed in the U.S. by SMITHMARK PUBLISHERS
a division of U.S. Media Holdings, Inc.,
16 East 32nd Street, New York, NY 10016

ISBN 0-7651-9256-X
8202

# Contents

# About this book

This book introduces you to the spooky subject of the supernatural – bizarre incidents and ghostly sightings beyond explanation.

It is hard to prove that ghosts exist, however many convincing stories have been told about them. People have reported seeing ghostly humans, animals and even machines. These ghosts are said to behave very strangely and scare people who see them, but are rarely reported to have caused actual harm.

From premonitions to poltergeists, to witches and werewolves, learn all about the unknown. Discover amazing stories about fortune telling and flying saucers, haunted houses and vampires, and things that go bump in the night!

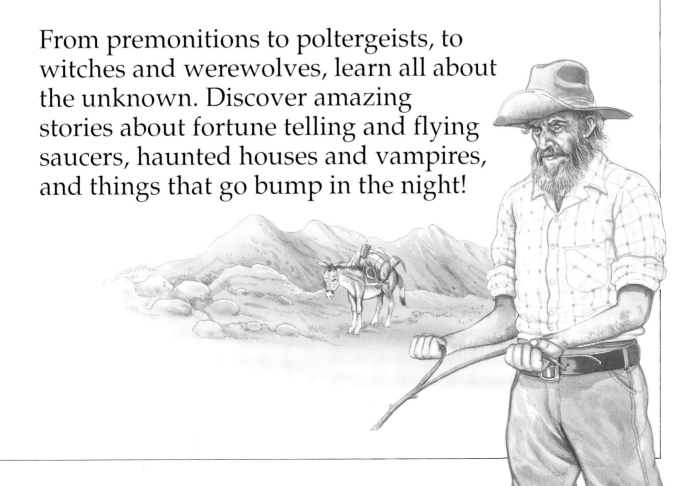

The existence of ghosts has never been proved scientifically. However throughout history many people have reported sightings of ghosts.

Ghosts are believed to be the spirits of people who have died, but sometimes they seem to resemble living people. There are animal ghosts and even ghostly ships, cars, planes and trains.

It is said that there have been many appearances of **royal ghosts.** King Henry VIII's beheaded wife, Anne Boleyn, is said to haunt the Tower of London, England. Two of his other wives roam the corridors at Hampton Court Palace.

In 1962, English brothers, Derek and Norman Ferguson claimed to have seen lots of **ghostly animals** while driving their car along a highway in Scotland.

A **bizarre bat** with a human head is a ghostly legend of Northern American Indians.

**Haunted computers** have been reported in many parts of the world.

**Glamis Castle**, the birthplace of Princess Margaret, is believed to be the most haunted royal building in Scotland. This 14th-century castle is said to be the home of a monster, a vampire and a whole host of ghosts.

Some people believe that ghosts like to haunt houses as well as ancient castles. In 1966, a British family had to be rehoused by their local government because they thought their house had been haunted for two years.

FOR SALE

# Ghosts around the world

There have been hundreds of ghostly sightings. Such stories have been reported from many countries around the globe.

Often these stories reflect the legends and traditions of the country in which the hauntings occur.

Over 150 years ago, a **Danish** man was wrongfully hanged for stealing. It is claimed that a shadowy outline of a body, hanging from a gallows, still appears today, just before the death of a family member.

One of the best known English ghosts is that of **Dick Turpin** who was famous for robbing travelers. He was a hero of the poor people because he stole from the wealthy. Turpin was hanged in 1739. It is widely believed that his ghost still appears on Hounslow Heath – now known as **Heathrow Airport**!

**Abraham Lincoln** was one of the most influential presidents of the United States. He was assassinated in April, 1865. It is said that every year during the month of April, the President's funeral train appears. It can be seen traveling along a stretch of track in New York State.

It is said that whenever the President's ghostly train appears, a complete military band can be heard blasting away.

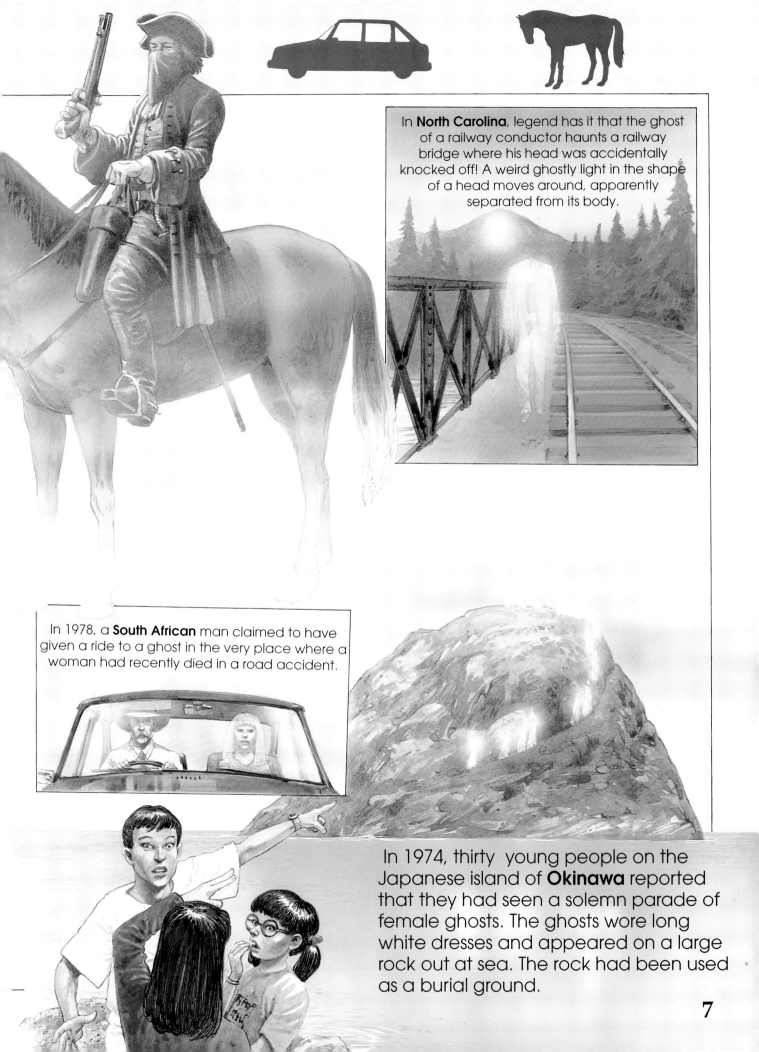

In **North Carolina**, legend has it that the ghost of a railway conductor haunts a railway bridge where his head was accidentally knocked off! A weird ghostly light in the shape of a head moves around, apparently separated from its body.

In 1978, a **South African** man claimed to have given a ride to a ghost in the very place where a woman had recently died in a road accident.

In 1974, thirty young people on the Japanese island of **Okinawa** reported that they had seen a solemn parade of female ghosts. The ghosts wore long white dresses and appeared on a large rock out at sea. The rock had been used as a burial ground.

# Poltergeists

A poltergeist is described as an invisible and noisy ghost. It is said that when a poltergeist is present people hear scratching, banging and mysterious voices. Sometimes fires start and strange smells fill the air.

Often poltergeists throw things around, smash ornaments and move heavy furniture. They are said to be invisible vandals!

In 1661, a magistrate confiscated a drum from a local beggar in **Tedworth**, England. Legend has it that a phantom drum could be heard frequently and lit candles floated up the chimney. The magistrate's horse was even found with its hind leg stuck in its mouth!

A family in **Barbados** buried deceased relatives in a big tomb. Each time the tomb was opened the coffins were found scattered around.

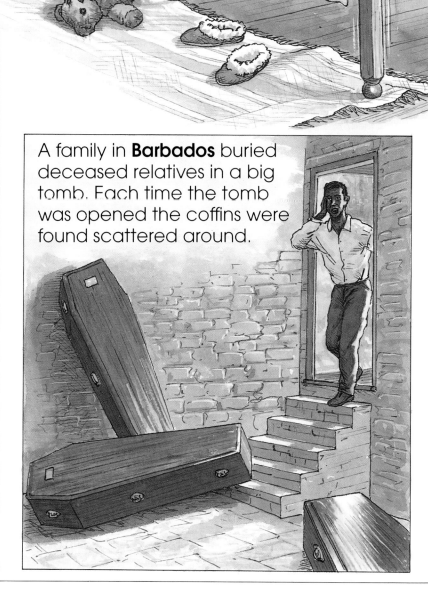

In 1960, an 11-year-old Scottish girl, **Virginia Campbell**, claimed she was being aggravated by a poltergeist for two months. It followed her wherever she went. One night her bed started shaking as if there was an earthquake. The haunting stopped once her parents held prayer meetings in their house.

Objects were said to fly around when a poltergeist made its home on a farm in **Lancashire**, England. A cow was even lifted to a hay loft. How it got there nobody knows – it certainly could not have climbed up the rickety ladder.

In 1951, a family reported strange happenings in their **London** home. A policeman found furniture being thrown across a room. Strangely, the violent activity stopped instantly once a light was turned on.

During 1967, a poltergeist started creating a disruption around 11-year-old **Matthew Manning** from Cambridge, England. Furniture began to move all over the family home and strange scratching noises could be heard. The haunting ended when Matthew began to create strange and beautiful drawings.

# Funny ghosts

It is said that ghosts like playing tricks. But ghosts and people seem to have a very different sense of humor. Often people do not find what ghosts do very funny. Ghosts are more likely to terrify people than make them laugh.

Over 60 years ago, on the Isle of Man in the Irish Sea, a ghostly **mongoose** was said to haunt an old farmhouse by the sea. It told jokes, sang songs and even swore. It told everyone its name was Gef. When the farmhouse was sold the new owner shot an unusual little furry animal. Gef has never been seen since.

Over 25 years ago, a derelict hotel in Wales was being demolished. Even though the electricity to the building had been cut off, the **elevator** kept on working.

Twelve-year-old English boy, **Michael Collingridge**, was recovering from tonsillitis when a walking stick in his bedroom appeared to dance. It jumped all around the room and began to tap out well-known tunes!

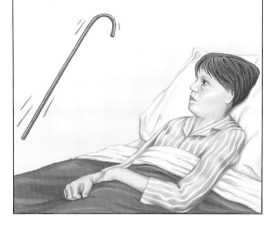

When the Pritchard family from **Pontefract** in Wales was plagued by a ghost, a woman from a Christian charity tried to drive the ghost away by singing *Onward Christian Soldiers*. The ghost responded by picking up her gloves and conducting her as she sang!

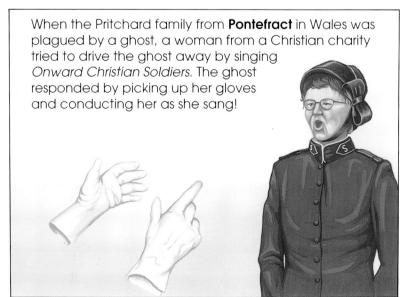

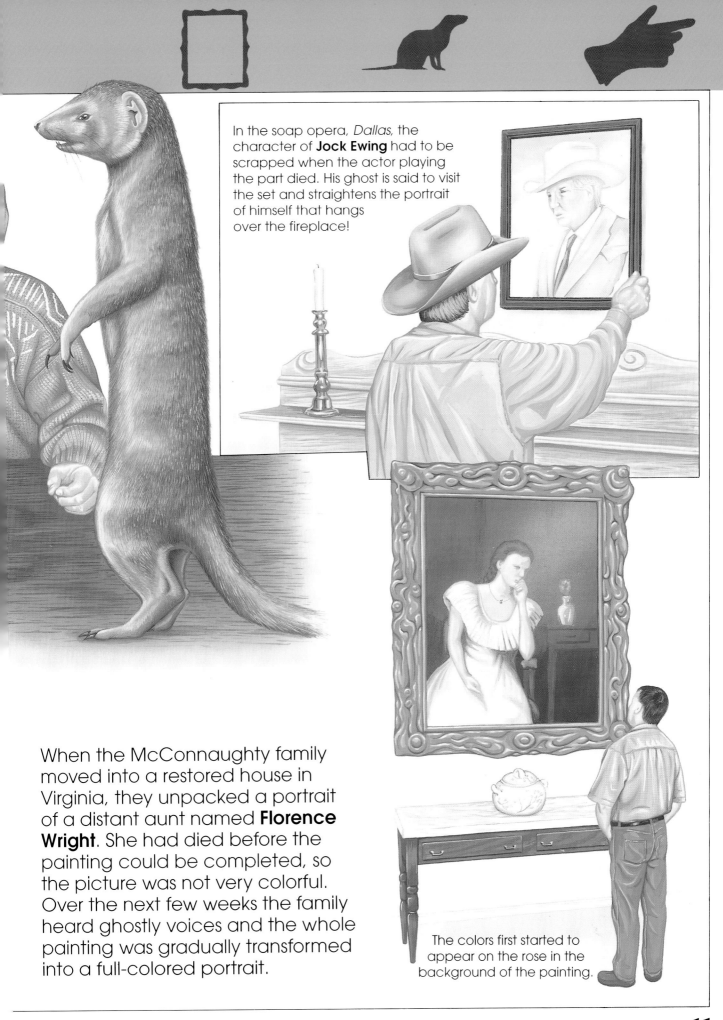

In the soap opera, *Dallas*, the character of **Jock Ewing** had to be scrapped when the actor playing the part died. His ghost is said to visit the set and straightens the portrait of himself that hangs over the fireplace!

When the McConnaughty family moved into a restored house in Virginia, they unpacked a portrait of a distant aunt named **Florence Wright**. She had died before the painting could be completed, so the picture was not very colorful. Over the next few weeks the family heard ghostly voices and the whole painting was gradually transformed into a full-colored portrait.

The colors first started to appear on the rose in the background of the painting.

# Haunted houses

It is said that haunted houses creak and ghosts glide through the walls.

It is believed that ghosts haunt places where they once lived, but no one knows if hauntings really happen!

Legend has it that **Ballechin House** in Scotland is haunted by invisible dogs who hit guests with their tails. It is also said to be home to ghostly nuns and a disembodied hand!

**Raynham Hall** in Norfolk, England, is thought to be haunted by the ghost of Dorothy Walpole who died there. In 1936, a photograph of a ghostly woman in a veil was snapped by a professional photographer visiting the hall.

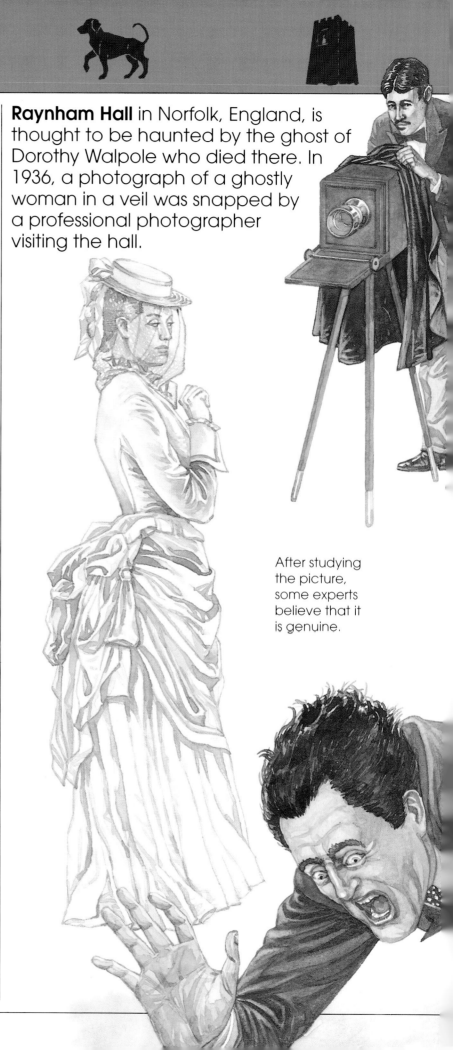

After studying the picture, some experts believe that it is genuine.

The most haunted house in Britain was said to be **Borley Rectory**. Even though it burnt down in 1939, poltergeists are said to haunt the ruins. Two headless ghosts and a phantom nun are also believed to have appeared.

The home of the British Prime Minister, **Number 10 Downing Street**, London, is said to be haunted by a politician from regency times.

Between 1883 and 1934, number **16 Montpelier Road** in London was the scene of twenty suicides and one murder. The victims had fallen from the top of the tower. In 1944, an investigator visited the house and was almost thrown from the tower himself. A photograph taken shows a ghost in Victorian clothing in an upstairs window!

People have invented all kinds of weird ways to ward off ghosts. Good luck charms and complicated rituals are used to scare ghosts away.

Inuits never remove someone who has died in an **igloo** through the front door. It is thought the spirit of the dead person would return if it knew where the front door was!

In China, the burning of **joss sticks** is thought to ward off unwanted spirits. Loud drums are beaten and noisy fireworks are set off at funerals to frighten away evil spirits.

14

Some people wear **amulets** and **talismans** (good luck charms) around their necks to scare off evil spirits and bring good fortune.

Some Asian communities will demolish the house someone has died in and then build a new home. It is believed that this gives the dead a resting place before finding **eternal peace**.

Many societies believe everyone has a **guardian spirit**. Mohammedans believe that we have four – two for the day and two for the night!

In many parts of the world it is still the custom to cover all the **mirrors** in a house until after a funeral. This protects against a spirit stealing the reflection of a living person and taking them off to the spirit world.

# Mysteries in the sky

Thousands of people have reported strange sights in the sky, from frogs to unidentified flying objects (UFOs).

There have even been stories of close encounters with aliens. As a result, many people are convinced that there is life beyond planet Earth.

The first reported sighting of a **UFO** was during the 1200s, long before the invention of the airplane!

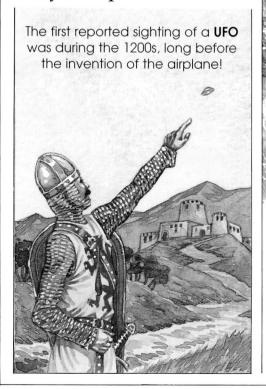

In 1975, a farmer in Switzerland sighted a **flying saucer**. Over the years he said he was visited by its three passengers called Somjasc, Ptaah and Asket. They told him that they were from the planet Erra, about 400 light years away.

In 1985, writer Whitley Strieber claimed that he had been abducted by **aliens** who gave him a thorough scientific examination. So disturbed was he by the experience that he sought the help of a hypnotist. Hypnosis revealed that he believed that aliens had been visiting him since childhood!

Numerous sightings of aliens have been reported in the **Broadhaven Triangle** in Wales. A luminous ball chased one car for miles. The occupants reached home to find a burnt-out television in their living room and a glowing figure in a silver suit in their garden.

In 1954, shoppers in Birmingham, England, were rained on by hundreds of tiny **frogs**! Many similar instances have been reported. Sometimes these are believed to be caused by supernatural forces.

In 1948, a **spacecraft** was reported to have crash-landed in New Mexico, United States. Eye-witnesses claimed that fourteen aliens were discovered on board the spacecraft. It has been said that the aliens were three feet tall and looked like humans with green, webbed feet.

# Mysterious disappearances

Throughout history there have been reports of people vanishing without trace. Ships and airplanes seem to have disappeared into thin air! Some of these cases are still shrouded in mystery.

Sometimes stories have been made up to explain disappearances. When famous band leader, **Glenn Miller**, vanished in 1944, some people believed that his face had been so disfigured in a plane crash that he had decided to hide away for the rest of his life.

The crew's meal was found half-eaten on the table.

In 1872, the entire crew of the merchant ship, the *Marie Celeste*, vanished. The ship was completely undamaged but no one aboard was ever seen again.

Often disappearances are hoaxes. In 1880, the story of a farmer who had apparently vanished hit the headlines in **Tennessee**. It turned out that a hardware salesman, who had been snowed into his house, had invented the whole story out of boredom!

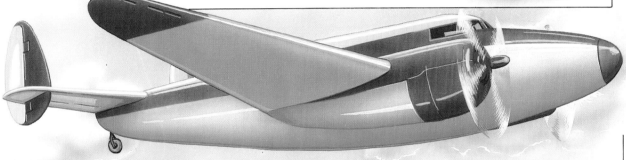

In 1937, **Amelia Earhart**, a record-breaking pilot, disappeared en route to an island in the Pacific Ocean. No one has ever been able to explain this mysterious disappearance.

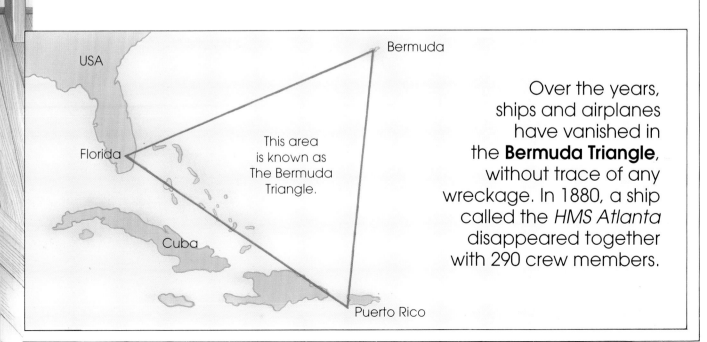

USA

Bermuda

Florida

This area is known as The Bermuda Triangle.

Cuba

Puerto Rico

Over the years, ships and airplanes have vanished in the **Bermuda Triangle**, without trace of any wreckage. In 1880, a ship called the *HMS Atlanta* disappeared together with 290 crew members.

# Witchcraft

Witchcraft comes from two old English words, *wita* and *craeft* which means craft of the wise. Some witches are thought to have special knowledge of the plants and herbs used to cure sickness.

In the past witches were thought to use their powers in an evil way.

In the past, anybody accused of **witchcraft** could be brought to trial. They were sometimes tortured until they had no option but to "confess."

Witchcraft was outlawed in the United Kingdom until 1951, when the old law was overturned. Today, it is quite legal to be a witch and join a **coven** or group of witches.

During 1692, in **Salem**, Massachusetts, a group of children accused 200 residents of being witches. The "witches" were brought to trial and 20 were executed. It was later agreed it had all been a terrible mistake.

At the time of the **winter solstice**, in December, witches perform "The Dance of the Wheel," a special ceremony to coax back the sun. They dance and leap around a boiling cauldron to represent the spring.

Traditional doctors in Africa used to be referred to as **witch doctors.** These doctors are expert herbalists and they sometimes call upon spirit powers to help cure their patients.

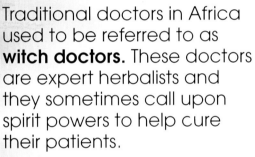

During the 1300s, the **Christian Church** formed a group called the **Inquisition** to find people who disagreed with the church, including witches. They falsely believed that "witches" made pacts with the devil, flew on broomsticks and even ate babies!

Many people believe that fortunetellers can look into the future. Some of them look at cards or tea leaves. Others look to the stars to see what lies ahead.

**Rune stones** are a set of 25 small tablets or stones which are believed to have special meaning. A rune reader can recognize what the stones represent according to the way they are laid out.

Most fortune telling methods originated in China. **I Ching** is an ancient Chinese book of knowledge which is believed to have the answer to everything!

No two hands are the same. **Palmists** read people's hands to predict how long they will live and even how many children they will have.

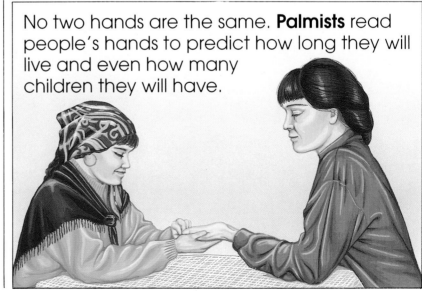

**Astrology** places people into twelve different groups which correspond with their birth dates. Maps of the stars and planets are consulted to forecast what the future holds.

**Phrenology** is the art of telling a fortune by feeling the bumps on a person's head.

Some people read their **horoscope** to predict what will happen during a day, week or month.

The Chinese invented **dominoes** as a method of predicting the future. The dominoes are put in a pouch, shaken and removed. Fortunes are read according to the position in which the dominoes are laid out.

23

# Second sight

Some people claim to have second sight. They believe that they see or sense things which are invisible to other people. Sometimes they even say that they can tell when a terrible event is about to happen.

In 1925, a famous palmist predicted that **Edward, Prince of Wales** would be forced to abdicate soon after he became King. Amazingly, 11 years later this premonition became fact!

In 1889, **Morgan Roberts** wrote *The Wreck of the Titan*. It tells the story of a massive luxury liner, called the *Titan*, which hit an iceberg and sank. The **Titanic** did exactly that 14 years later and hundreds of the passengers were drowned.

In May 1979, an American called **David Booth** dreamed of a terrible air crash. He informed the airline but they took no notice of him. The next day an airplane crashed at the Chicago airport killing 273 people.

**Jeane Dixon**, an American who claims to have powers of second sight, warned that the President would be assassinated. Eventually, on November 23, 1963, she told friends that the day had come.
**John F. Kennedy** was shot dead that afternoon.

The police have often been helped by people with second sight. **Gerald Croiset** spent his life helping Danish police to find murderers and to locate missing people and buried bodies.

It is said that some people are gifted with bizarre powers. They claim to be able to make things rise above the ground and objects change shape all by themselves.

**Astral projection** is when a person feels that their spirit is rising out of their actual body. Such people claim that while sleeping they can sit on the end of their bed and watch themselves.

Many people believe that **dowsers** can sense where gold and oil are hidden in the ground. They use instruments, such as bent metal rods or forked twigs, which tremble or rotate when they have found the hidden treasure.

**Levitation** is said to defy the law of gravity by making bodies or objects rise and float in the air. Some eastern holy men are supposed to be able to levitate themselves at will.

Experts are unable to explain the strange pictures created by psychic photography.

It is claimed that **psychic photography** is the ability to take photographs of thoughts. Ted Serios from Chicago believed that when he took a photograph of his face an image in his thoughts would appear on the film!

**Psychokinesis** is the ability to affect objects by mental means alone. **Uri Geller** from Israel, for example, is famous for bending keys. He has even claimed to be able to stop a cable car in midair. Many magicians believe he is a fraud.

# Strange and bizarre

For hundreds of years sightings of strange creatures, mysterious monsters and bizarre landmarks have been reported all over the world. Even today experts are unable to find scientific explanations for many of these mysteries.

**Bigfoot – or Sasquatch –** is described as a tall, hairy monster that lives in Washington State. A Bigfoot sighting is reported regularly so there must be lots of these monsters!

**Yeti**, or the **Abominable Snowman** is thought to be a tall, white, furry monster. The first sighting was reported in Tibet in 1921 and there have been numerous reports of appearances ever since.

Enormous, elaborate shapes known as **crop circles** have appeared in the crop fields of Hampshire and Wiltshire, England. No one is sure how they are formed or where they came from although many explanations have been suggested.

It is said that the **Pyramids** in Egypt are surrounded by strange powers. Plants apparently grow faster and it is even claimed that people are filled with amazing energy around the Pyramids!

Nowadays modern technology, from radar to the latest computers, is used to investigate sightings of unknown creatures.

The **Loch Ness Monster** is believed to be a gigantic prehistoric reptile which still survives in Loch Ness, Scotland. Sightings of it have been reported as long ago as 565 B.C. Although there are numerous photographs, the existence of this "monster" has never really been proved.

# More spooky cases

Tradition has it that when a dramatic event has occurred, ghostly phantoms will return to haunt the place where the disturbing incident happened.

Here are two especially chilling phantom stories.

During the 1600s, the owner of **Bettiscombe Manor** in Dorset, England cruelly enslaved an African man and brought him back to England. The slave said that if he was not buried in his homeland he would return to haunt the manor. The slave's request was ignored and he was buried in the local churchyard.

It is said that such terrible screaming could be heard in the churchyard that the owner was forced to dig up the coffin and put it in the loft of Bettiscombe Manor.

The skull remains at Bettiscombe Manor and seems to guard it. If the skull is taken outside, it is said that screams shake the house.

**The Flying Dutchman** was a ship which sank in the 1600s. Its ghost is said to haunt the oceans. In 1881 the crew of *HMS Inconstant* thought they saw the ship.

In 1939, over 100 people claimed to have seen the ship as they sunbathed on a beach near Cape Town, South Africa.

In 1911, the crew of the steamer, *Orkney Belle*, encountered **The Flying Dutchman**. It was totally deserted. It is said that three bells were heard and the ghost ship vanished into the fog.

During World War II, a German admiral reported that the crew of his U-Boat submarine had seen the phantom ship.

**31**

# Index